Homeless Outreach
& Housing First:
Lessons Learned

Jay S. Levy, MSW, LICSW

Loving Healing Press

ISBN-13: 978-1-61599-136-5 paperback
eISBN: 978-1-61599-137-2 eBook

Published by
Loving Healing Press
5145 Pontiac Trail
Ann Arbor, MI 48105

Tollfree USA/CAN: 888-761-6268
FAX: 734-663-6861

www.LHPress.com
info@LHPress.com

Distributed by Ingram

Confidentiality

The homeless narrative depicted in this work is based on actual persons and events from my experiences as an outreach counselor. However, names, places, and events have been altered to protect client confidentiality.

About the Cover

The Westfield (MA) Safe Havens Project
Mental Health Association Inc. Springfield, MA.

HUD and the Commonwealth of Massachusetts jointly fund this six-unit Safe Havens project. The house provides permanent housing with supports for chronically homeless adults with a severe and persistent mental illness. The Safe Havens model has proven to be a valuable resource in the region's 'housing first' approach to homelessness. To effectively implement a housing first strategy, the region has recognized the need for a wide range of housing options, including the Safe Havens model.

Cover photo and written description by David Modzelewski, Mental Health Association, Inc., Springfield, MA

Contents

Dedication

I dedicate this project (monograph) to people without homes, and to all those who have survived homelessness, and to the outreach workers who help the most vulnerable among us. May their courage, strength and dedication serve as an inspiration to others.

Special Thanks

I am indebted to my wife Louise, and my daughters, Talia and Sara for their love, patience, playfulness, and wisdom.

I'd like to thank my friend, David Modzelewski for his continued insight and photographic genius.

Portions of this monograph have previously appeared in *Recovering The Self: A Journal of Hope and Healing* published by LH Press. Thanks to Victor Volkman and Ernest Dempsey for encouraging my writing and granting permission to reprint these articles.

Proceeds from the Monograph

The Author has pledged 15% of royalties and other related profits, to a 501c(3) charity that supports the cause of ending chronic homelessness.

Introduction

There is a fundamental relationship between *homeless outreach* and *housing first*. Homeless outreach is an essential step toward meeting people experiencing long-term or episodic (multiple episodes) homelessness and developing the critical trusting relationships necessary for supporting transitions to affordable housing and/or needed treatment. The greater our success in implementing *housing first*, the more our need for high quality support services that promote housing stabilization. Over time we have seen a critical shift. Some of the formerly hardest to reach folks are now successfully housed, but still have chronic medical, mental health, and substance abuse issues that negatively impact their overall sense of health and wellbeing, including their ability to effectively connect with their neighbors and community.

Whether we are providing homeless outreach or housing stabilization services for people with longstanding difficulties, the central challenges remain the same. This is particularly relevant to people who are either formerly or currently chronically homeless, while being reluctant to participate in treatment and/or recovery based options. What is needed is a pretreatment approach. *Pretreatment* (Levy, 2010) *is an approach that enhances safety while promoting transition to housing (e.g. housing first options), and/or treatment alternatives through client centered supportive interventions that develop goals and motivation to create positive change.*

There are five basic pretreatment principles (See Pretreatment Principles Chart on p. 3) that can guide our work:

- Relationship Formation – Promote trust via Stages of Engagement
- Common Language Construction – Develop effective communication
- Ecological Considerations – Support the process of transition and adaptation
- Facilitate Change – Utilize Stages of Change and Motivational Interviewing
- Promote Safety – Apply Crisis Intervention and Harm reduction Strategies

This monograph not only explores the relationship between *homeless outreach* and *housing first*, but also highlights what we've learned. Basic truths are reinforced like the importance of a client-centered relationship, the need for affordable housing, and the essential combination of affordable housing and support services for promoting housing stabilization. It also explores both subtle and intricate aspects of helping by applying pretreatment principles of care.

I present three different modalities to express what I know: A journal article that highlights important research and philosophical considerations, storytelling via

Ronald's Narrative: The Original Housing First, as well as my recent interview for *Recovering The Self: A Journal of Hope and Healing*. These three documents are brought together in an effort provide a rich and fertile educational resource for learning and reflection. I hope the reader finds value in these different approaches to disseminating critical information that both encourages and informs needed action. Our objective is to help the most vulnerable among us achieve a sense of community, dignity and meaning, while living safely in their homes.

Pretreatment Principles & Applications*

Principle	Application
Enhance Safety	• Engage with homeless individuals in order to reduce the risk of harm and enhance safety (e.g. provide blankets on cold night) • Stabilize acute symptoms via crisis intervention and utilize opportunity for further work
Relationship Formation	• Attempt to engage with homeless people in a manner that promotes trust, safety, & autonomy, while developing relevant goals • Stages include: Pre-Engagement, Engagement, Contracting (Levy, 1998)
Common Language Construction	• Attempt to understand a homeless person's world by learning the meaning of his or her gestures, words and actions • Promote mutual understanding & jointly define goals • Stages include: Understanding, Utilizing, and Bridging Language (Levy, 2004)
Promote & Support Change	• Prepare clients to achieve and maintain positive change by exploring ambivalence, reinforcing healthy behaviors, developing skills, as well as needed supports • Utilize Change Model & Motivational Interviewing Principles
Cultural & Ecological Considerations	• Prepare and support clients for the process of transition and adaptation to new relationships, ideas, services, resources, treatment, and housing

*A *Pretreatment Model* integrates basic concepts from the *Change Model* (Prochaska & DiClemente,1982), *Motivational Interviewing* (Miller & Rollnick,1991, *Ecological Social Work* (Germain & Gitterman, 1980), and *Narrative Psychology* (Epston & White, 1992).

The Case for Housing First: Moral, Fiscal, and Quality of Life Reasons for Ending Chronic Homelessness

There is a heavy price tag for long-term homelessness. It is not only a societal ill, but also has a negative impact on the health and welfare of the many individuals experiencing chronic homelessness. Wasserman and Clair (2010) state, "…addressing homelessness is literally a matter of life and death, as it is associated with all sorts of health outcomes such as addiction, mental illness, chronic and acute disease, malnutrition and violence." For many years, while providing outreach-counseling services, I witnessed this on the streets and in the shelters of New York City, Boston, and Western MA. Unfortunately, it was not unusual to meet people living on the fringes of our society without any sense of hope or expectation for the comforts of a better life. Throughout the 1980s, 90s and much of the new millennium, the response to homelessness has been primarily geared toward helping people who are most ready to accept services and programming, as well as providing temporary shelter for those who could soon return to work. In the meantime, long-term homelessness has become an all too common and accepted reality. In fact, research has shown that on a yearly basis 2.3 – 3.5 million people are homeless (Burt and Aron, 2000). Further, as much as 20 percent of the homeless population (Kuhn and Culhane, 1998) are either among the long-term homeless, or have had multiple episodes of homelessness.

This is at the core of the Department of Housing and Urban Development's (HUD) definition, which defines *chronic homelessness* (McKinney-Vento, 2002) as an individual with disability (addiction, mental or medical illness) who has been homeless for at least 12 consecutive months or has had at least 4 distinct episodes of homelessness within a three-year period. While economic realities that include unemployment, underemployment, and lack of affordable housing are amid the initial causes that can lead to chronic homelessness, other significant variables consist of major mental illness and/or addiction and other medical issues that compromise social and vocational functioning. In fact, many shelters that have prided themselves in becoming safe havens for the poor and less fortunate have also become default institutions for long-term homeless persons with acute and chronic health issues. Meanwhile, among the many myths is that people who experience chronic homelessness are unworkable or disinterested in getting help, or simply prefer their homeless life style. Unfortunately, the costs of writing off a significant proportion of the homeless population has been staggering. Misguided homelessness policies have led to both moral and fiscal concerns, while the quality of life slowly deteriorates among the homeless themselves, as well as throughout our cities and towns.

Mortality, Health, and Moral Considerations

Somehow we have convinced ourselves that people who are long-term homeless with mental illness, addiction, and/or major medical conditions need to seek treatment prior to getting housed. In many instances we have turned this into a litmus test by declaring treatment as a prerequisite for residential placement. While this has motivated some people to begin needed treatment, others have refused treatment and have thus suffered dire consequences. The stark reality is that our attempts to avoid "enabling" have led to far too many deaths. While we wait for chronically homeless persons to hit bottom and request treatment, higher numbers continue to die. Dr. Hwang, Dr. O'Connell and colleagues (1998) studied the vulnerability of particular homeless subgroups and found that people who were unsheltered or living outside for at least 6 months were at high risk of death if they fell into any of the following categories:

- Triple diagnosis of mental illness, substance abuse, medical condition
- 60 years of age or older
- History of Frostbite, hypothermia, or trench foot
- At least 3 emergency room visits over the prior 3 months
- More than three hospitalizations or emergency room visits in a year
- Diagnosis of HIV/AIDS, liver or renal disease

Over a five year period, 40% of the people who were among these categories died and the average age of death was 47 (O'Connell, 2005). It is equally clear that a high proportion (at least 46%) of homeless individuals sheltered and unsheltered suffer from chronic medical conditions ranging from arthritis, hernias and foot ulcers to liver, renal, and heart disease (Burt, et al., 1999). These health issues, as well as chronic mental illness and addiction, are only exacerbated by unsafe, substandard living conditions that lack basic access to food, clean clothes, sanitary bathroom facilities and a secure place to sleep. When one considers the impact of unstable and chaotic environments on health issues, it's hard to fathom why health care professionals and residential programs serving *at risk* homeless individuals have often prioritized compliance with treatment above housing placement (Levy, 2010, p. 15). It is a given that successful treatment is often dependent upon living conditions that promote, rather than diminish, health and safety.

After considering the serious ramifications of a *treatment first*, rather than a *housing first* approach, one may conclude that it is a moral imperative to house vulnerable chronically homeless persons as quickly as possible, while continuing outreach and support services. It is important to keep in mind that housing is not an end in itself, but rather an opportunity to continue our efforts to build pathways to needed treatment services and community resources.

Financial Considerations

The cost of long-term homelessness impacts us on many fronts. Just consider that every day someone resides in a homeless shelter there is a cost for the bed and the staff needed to assure their safety. Surprisingly, the cost for a shelter bed in NYC can run as high as $19,800 per year (Culhane and Metraux, 2008). In addition, the longer someone is homeless, the more likely a person will experience untreated medical, mental health and addiction issues. This not only leads to periodic crises for police, EMTs and emergency room staff, but also results in multiple hospitalizations. In other words, long-term homelessness leads to acute medical, psychiatric and addiction issues being managed and treated via shelters, emergency rooms and inpatient facilities at an extremely high cost (Kuhn and Culhane, 1998). Malcolm Gladwell (2006) wrote a compelling article in the New Yorker that tells the story of Million Dollar Murray. Murray consumed large amounts of alcohol, while living on the streets of Reno, Nevada. From time to time Murray would get sober, clean himself up and resume employment. However, without needed support services, he would relapse and end up back on the streets. Inevitably, Murray suffered a number of chronic and acute medical issues leading to multiple hospitalizations. The cost over a ten-year period added up to more than a million dollars! This price tag did not even factor in police, EMT, and other emergency services that were separate from the local hospital bill. The problem is that there is more than one Murray! There are actually a high number of unsheltered individuals going in and out of emergency rooms, detoxification facilities, and hospitals throughout our cities and towns. A five-year study of chronically homeless persons (O'Connell, et al., 2005) found that 119 street dwellers accounted for 18,384 emergency room visits and 871 medical hospitalizations. The average annual health care cost for individuals living on the street was $28,436 compared to $6,056 for individuals who were successfully placed in housing.

Fortunately, *housing first* options comprised of affordable housing with support staff costs considerably less than the status quo. The expenditure for subsidized housing and support services ranges from $12,000 – $20,000 per year, as compared to our significantly higher price tag for inaction. While *housing first* programs are no guarantee against relapse, there is a proven track record of significantly reducing medical costs and maintaining people in permanent housing (Home and Healthy for Good Report, 2010; Stefancic and Tsemberis, 2007). The financial case for providing housing with support services to at risk or vulnerable chronically homeless individuals is clear. In addition, advocates, policy makers and providers now realize that the same argument can be made for serving long-term homeless families. Overall, the evidence shows that housing with support services not only saves lives, but is also a financially wise practice.

Quality of Life Considerations

Arguably it is basic things like good health, nutritious food, a secure home, livable income, and positive relationships that are among the ingredients toward attaining a better quality of life. Successful homeless outreach begins with the challenge of building a positive relationship and offering basic need items such as food and a warm blanket, as well as access to safe shelter and/or affordable housing. Unfortunately, chronic homelessness and the growing effects of poverty have had a negative impact on the quality of life throughout our society. In many places across our country, the poor and the rich live side by side with an ever-shrinking middle class. This is expressed quite vividly in the homeless realm. I have spent much time meeting people who are impoverished and without homes next to Boston's high end stores along Newbury St., or beside New York City's Upper West Side's cafes. The irony of such a meeting is shared by all of us. Places like NYC's Port Authority and Boston's South Station have become safe havens for the homeless, while commuters generally make efforts to avoid eye contact or any kind of human connection. Even in smaller towns throughout Western MA, business owners register complaints of homeless individuals blocking their entryways and/or frightening away customers. Further, many cities and towns have struggled with how to respond to aggressive panhandling practices. Finally, it is not unusual for families to feel uncomfortable or unsafe visiting certain parks or playgrounds because a person experiencing long-term homelessness has taken up residence there. While it is true that homelessness may not be the main cause of these problems, it is understandable why many people feel inconvenienced or even threatened by their homeless neighbors. Though it is tempting to turn this into a dichotomy of us vs. them, it is clear that we are in this together. In fact, it is this type of dualistic thinking that has led to unsuccessful homelessness policies and flawed interventions. Ignoring people who are homeless, punishing them, or worse yet, treating them as second-class citizens will not resolve this thorny issue. Obviously, people without homes directly suffer the consequences including poor health and a degraded quality of life, but this is also a societal ill that affects us all. Therefore, we must find a way to address this on both individual and societal levels.

Effective Pretreatment Strategies

Homeless outreach

Over time, the world of a person experiencing long-term homelessness gets more and more defined by meeting immediate needs such as finding food and shelter, staying warm, and may even include ongoing efforts to feed addiction, rather than continually searching for work and affordable housing. Anyone who has experienced long-term unemployment understands the internal struggle of maintaining hope when the prospects of success continually appear grim. Many people who experience long-term homelessness are hesitant to trust others and have found a sense of meaning that reflects their culture, individuality, and homeless circumstance, while upholding their personal values and need for freedom and safety. These survival strategies, meaning making, and clinging to strongly held beliefs and values, form an integral part of the adaptation to the traumatic experiences of homelessness. The central challenge of outreach (See 10 Golden Rules list, p. 11) is to develop a trusting relationship that respects the autonomy of the individual, as well as speaking a language that consists of shared words, ideas, and values (Levy, 2004). This is at the heart of a pretreatment approach, which is governed by the following cardinal rule: Meet clients where they are at! The relationship is the foundation of pretreatment work, while common language development is its main tool (Levy, 2010). It is from the safety of a trusting relationship and the development of a common language that makes it possible to offer potential resources and services that resonate well in the world of the homeless person. Ironically, the outreach worker is often struggling to access the very resources and services that their clients need most; namely income and afford-able housing with support services!

Housing First

It is essential that we directly connect affordable housing and support service options to outreach teams and shelter staff, so that it can be readily available to persons experiencing chronic homelessness. If we really want to resolve long-term homelessness, we need to offer accessible, affordable housing alternatives with support services. This includes a very broad-based eligibility criterion that is inclusive rather than exclusive. *Housing first* does not require that a person partake in mental health, addiction program or medical treatment; or that they achieve sobriety *prior* to being housed. The basic premise is that people should be housed as quickly as possible with support services that can develop pathways and/or bridges to community resources, services and treatment. The only thing required to enter a *housing first* apartment is a designation of chronic homelessness or high vulnerability and a willingness to accept an outreach support service. Throughout the Western MA area, we have developed the Regional Engagement and Assessment of Chronically Homeless Housing First Program (REACH). This program not only attaches affordable housing options directly to outreach workers, but then directly involves the outreach workers in providing ongoing support services to newly housed individuals. This is a relationship-centered model that supports transitions to needed housing, resources and services. Other important tasks for outreach staff include providing advocacy with landlords, as well as rapid response to any issue that may threaten safety and/or permanent housing. The need for rapid response falls under four basic categories:

1. Non-payment of Rent
2. Conflict with Neighbors

3. Destruction of property

4. Personal Safety of tenant

If a person were once again to experience homelessness due to eviction or prematurely leaving their apartment, the homeless outreach process can easily resume. However, now the outreach team and hopefully the person re-experiencing homelessness have a chance to get perspective on the challenges of housing stabilization. Lessons learned from previous housing first attempts serve as a catalyst to renew our efforts to rapidly re-house the person who is in dire need of a safe and secure residence with support services. *Housing first* efforts have been tried in many cities throughout the country including Philadelphia, Boston, New York City, Las Vegas, and Seattle. Multiple studies have confirmed successful outcomes such as better than 84% housing retention rates, as well as reducing overall health care costs (Home and Healthy for Good Report, 2010; Stefancic and Tsemberis, 2007). The same pretreatment approach used to promote successful outreach can also be used to continue the work with newly housed individuals. This means that the residential outreach support services should continue to emphasize the basic pretreatment principles of relationship building, common language development, support transitions to needed resources and services, promote safety through harm reduction and crisis intervention, as well as facilitate and support positive change (Levy, 2000). Whether or not a particular *housing first* program is run as a scattered site or congregate living model, it is essential that the support service component is well developed and responsive to the immediate needs of the tenant, landlord and neighbors. This also means providing the right level and intensity of support services based on the willingness and needs of the individual.

Conclusion

Housing first initiatives and *Pretreatment* approaches consisting of outreach and engagement services have been proven and effective strategies toward reducing the financial and moral costs of chronic homelessness. This is not meant to minimize the importance of homelessness policies and overall systemic strategies needed to address the development of jobs, employment programs, and affordable housing, as well as promoting access to an array of needed services and resources. In fact, in many regions across the country, continua of care and Homeless Service Networks have formed with plans to end chronic homelessness. In many places, important steps have already been taken to integrate current services and resources, while targeting future funds to address the need for affordable housing and support services (e.g. All Roads Lead Home-The Pioneer Valley's Plan to End Homelessness, 2008). This article provides moral, fiscal, and quality of life reasons for both continuing and spreading these important efforts. One of the great challenges that lies ahead is to successfully transition from a shelter-based system of care to one that emphasizes front end affordable housing options. However, we need to be careful that we don't rush to close shelters prematurely and thereby put people at undue risk. I am reminded of the pitfalls of the deinstitutionalization movement during the 60s, when we rushed to close psychiatric hospitals, before having an adequate system of housing and support services in place. We don't want to make the same mistake in regard to homelessness policies. While *housing first* is an important tool, it doesn't resolve the underlying economic issues and dynamics that cause homelessness. The emergency shelter system may need to play the critical role of keeping people safe for the foreseeable future. In the end, we all benefit from a society that has come to grips with the negative impact of homelessness and the importance of eradicating chronic homelessness. The goal of ending chronic home-lessness is not only a fiscally sound policy that saves lives and provides a better quality of life for all of us, but it is also the right thing to do.

10 Golden Rules of Outreach Counseling (Pretreatment Perspective)

1. Meet clients (both literally and figuratively) where they are at!
2. The relationship is most important — Promote trust and respect autonomy.
3. Develop a common language of shared words, ideas and values.
4. Be goal centered — Join the person in setting goals that resonate well in his or her world.
5. Mutually define or characterize particular difficulties to achieving goals and jointly develop strategies or plans.
6. Carefully support transitions to new ideas, relationships (stages of engagement), environments (desensitization), and treatment (bridge client language to treatment language).
7. Promote Safety via Harm Reduction strategies and Crisis Intervention techniques.
8. Utilize crisis as an opportunity to promote positive change.
9. Respect the process of change — understand its stages and relevant interventions.
10. Understand the person's narrative and integrate a process of "meaning making" with movement toward positive change.

Ronald's Narrative: The Original Housing First

"Think of it this way, if you had valuable information… I mean something really valuable like the cure to a deadly disease. What would others do to bring you down?"

-Ronald

During the autumn of 1992, before the term *housing first* was widely used, I did outreach at a homeless shelter in Boston, Massachusetts. This is not to say that outreach counselors did not periodically try to quickly house chronically homeless individuals with significant disabilities including untreated mental illness and addiction. We did, and the results were decidedly mixed. One could argue whether or not this was truly *housing first*. After all, we didn't have prescribed housing stabilization services and the housing was not always subsidized or readily available. Instead, we simply did the best we could through our continued efforts to provide outreach and housing placement to those most in need. Just as importantly, there was very little support and acceptance of this practice. We made the decision to prioritize housing out of a deep-seated concern. We grew tired of being told that our clients weren't ready to enter independent housing or didn't qualify for residential programs. People in dire need were turned away for not meeting eligibility requirements such as six months of continuous sobriety, or not matching the right diagnostic category. Other times, our clients adamantly refused to enter programs or participate in treatment and therefore remained homeless and vulnerable to a variety of major health concerns. Outreach workers across America took chances out of necessity.

This is the story of the original *housing first*, as expressed through Ronald's narrative: how the best ideas can arise from the midst of our day-to-day challenges. As with any good story, we are taken on a journey that divulges much more than the title implies.

Pre-engagement

Ronald, an African American male in his mid-thirties, sat at the dinner table seemingly oblivious to the bleak and noisy environment of the homeless shelter. He slowly rocked his head forward and backward with a close-eyed grin and an impish laugh. He did this repeatedly, like some odd kind of ritual, while simultaneously finishing his snack of potato chips. Most of the chips made it into his mouth, though several crumbs escaped onto his straggly unkempt beard. I casually walked over to his table and pulled up a chair. Ronald continued with his repetitive behavior and showed no real response to my close proximity. I could smell the stale stench of alcohol and noticed the evidence of a recent outside nap: his partially torn and faded gray tee shirt had some old blades of grass mixed with small brown crackly leaves clinging to it. A bit more disturbingly, a small black bug quickly sprinted across Ronald's forehead before returning to the confines of his curly black hair. Despite feeling a bit reticent, I gave my best efforts to greet him in a friendly and non-threatening manner. For a brief moment Ronald responded with a one-word acknowledgement, before quickly resuming his focus on his internal world. Although I felt a little stuck, squarely in the pre-engagement phase (See Stages of Engagement chart on p. 26), I was hopeful of beginning a new and interesting relationship. Ronald was definitely aware of my presence, but rather than make an attempt at forced conversation, I felt the best strategy was to try again on a different day. I normally visited the shelter three nights a week to provide outreach-counseling services, so there would be other opportunities.

Over the next two weeks, I approached Ron on three separate occasions. My first two attempts met a similar fate. Ronald appeared much more interested in upholding his privacy, and showed little or no interest in conversing with me. My third approach was guided by the anonymous homeless outreach adage: "If you want to get to someone's head begin with their feet." I offered Ronald a new pair of socks! This immediately got his attention. I introduced myself as a homeless out-reach worker and asked Ronald if there was anything else that he needed. Ronald smiled and said that he was all set, yet very appreciative for receiving the socks. I left him with a pamphlet that listed meals, shelters, clothes, and medical services for the immediate area. We successfully met the challenge of the pre-engagement stage (Levy, 1998, Levy 2000) by establishing a welcomed communication with an initial sense of trust and safety.

Engagement & Contracting

During our next encounter, Ronald and I reviewed the pamphlet. He mentioned that he had been homeless for many years and already knew most of the area's service and resource options. He even cued me in on a meal program that was not listed. I thanked him for the information and promised to pass it on to others in need. At the end of our meeting, I quickly mentioned that we could see if he qualified for benefits ranging from food stamps to emergency assistance and Social Security. Ronald didn't say much, so I stated, "We could always talk about this or other ways of getting income at another time." Ron looked up and said, "That'd be fine." Though it wasn't very clear how he perceived my offer, further contact around assessing Ron's eligibility for benefits was a distinct possibility. At least our conversation ended with the expectation of further meetings. Our challenge, which is central to the engagement process (Levy, 1998, Levy 2000), was to form an ongoing welcomed communication that promotes trust and respects individual autonomy, so that Ron could be empowered toward discussing and setting goals.

Approximately three days later, I approached Ronald at the shelter. He was once again sitting alone and laughing to himself, while rocking his body back and forth. I asked if he had any thoughts about my offer to look into benefits or other ways to establish an income. Ron now showed improved eye contact and in a very sincere voice said that he really appreciated my concern, but didn't want to be a bother. He also stated that he was currently focused on finding a place to live, though he did not indicate a need for my assistance. Ron now showed greater connection. He was more easily engaged in conversation and expressed an interest in finding a residence. Considering that I had not yet observed him talking with others, this level of engagement seemed significant. I thought about an immediate offer to fill out housing applications, but didn't want to push things too fast and thereby appear overly directive. Instead, I clearly stated that he was not at all a bother and reinforced that my work (defining roles) was centered on helping people to pursue their goals inclusive of affordable housing.

Afterward, I reflected on Ronald's world. He seemed to value his privacy and showed indications of considerable difficulty connecting with others. He came across as exceedingly polite and concerned about being a "bother" to others. His mental status reflected both substance abuse and mental health issues as evidenced by the smell of alcohol on his breath, as well as his level of isolation, talking to himself and his repetitive rocking back and forth behaviors. In addition, he was among the hardcore homeless, meaning that he had been homeless for a long period of time and it was not unusual for him to sleep outside. While there was a great deal that I didn't know about Ronald's interests, strengths and difficulties, it was already clear to me that our continued engagement would remain tenuous unless we developed goals that could serve to motivate and invest Ron in our meetings. We were in need of a guiding purpose that could resonate well in his world, even if this differed from my initial inclination to help with applying for benefits or offering a treatment referral.

A couple of days later, I approached Ronald at the shelter and he greeted me with a boisterous voice and with a greater sense of confidence and control. His repetitive behaviors of rocking back and forth in isolation were gone. It was evident that this was at the expense of some very recent alcohol and possibly drug intake. He was inebriated and this helped him to be more forthright with his communication. I told Ron that he appeared much calmer and more outgoing and then directly asked, "Do you have any ideas as to why things are so different?" Ron smiled and said, "I recently took my medicine (slang for drugs)." I laughed knowingly and said, "You mean 'un-prescribed' medication!" Ron nodded in agreement before going on to share some of his frustrations over being homeless and impoverished. He reported having been homeless for at least five years and said that he really would like to get off the streets as quickly as possible. He explained that he didn't feel comfortable at the shelter, or particularly safe when he slept outside. I reflected back, "It sounds like times are hard" and then mentioned that we could look for affordable housing options. Ronald pulled out of his back pocket a worn and crumpled flyer on local housing resources. Together we reviewed the flyer, much like our previous review of the pamphlet on meals and shelters, except this time he initiated the review. After several approaches and three follow up meetings, we were now on the cusp of contracting for services. Ron had clearly requested help with a housing search and we ended our meeting with a plan to apply for subsidized housing. My hope was that the goal of finding affordable housing would be a natural conduit toward exploring his need for income, as well as understanding the potential benefits of mental health and substance abuse treatment.

Contracting and Re-contracting

Ronald and I met again at the shelter to fill out some forms for subsidized housing. The shelter was incredibly noisy and several shelter guests were intoxicated and rambunctious. Ron was once again high and had difficulty focusing on our paperwork. Nevertheless, we made it through one housing application before losing gumption due to his lethargy and lack of focus. I asked, "Do you think your un-prescribed medication has something to do with your low energy level?" Ron was silent for several seconds before sharing a sense of desperation, "Living at this shelter makes it impossible for me! I needed something to calm my nerves!" I went on to explain, "Considering the wait for subsidized housing could take several months, you might want to think about a quicker, safer, and more private alternative to the shelter." We left off with the understanding that we would explore these possibilities, while filling out additional housing forms during our next meeting. He agreed to meet the following morning at my local downtown office, which would be considerably quieter than the shelter. Ron and I made some initial progress with the development of a common language. We focused on safety and privacy issues, as well as finding a mutually acceptable way to refer to his alcohol and drug use as "un-prescribed medication." Ronald even shared some useful mental health terminology, when he referred to the need to calm his nerves. Another promising development was our agreement to meet at my office. This would afford us the opportunity to work on things earlier in the day away from the amped up shelter environment, and hopefully prior to his heavy drug and/or alcohol use.

I waited at my office for over an hour and Ron was a "no show." At around two in the afternoon I heard a gentle knock on my door. It was Ronald! He appeared a bit shaky, and very quiet... generally ill at ease. He presented as anxious and depressed, while being very apologetic for his lateness. I didn't smell any alcohol and could not tell if he was high, but wondered if I saw evidence of withdrawal. I picked up on the here and now and asked how it felt trying to get to our scheduled meeting. Ron expressed extreme difficulty with the task. He felt very anxious when traveling and was not comfortable entering unfamiliar buildings or riding in elevators. As he spoke, his body began to tremble and he appeared genuinely upset.

I commented on how over our last two meetings he sometimes appeared less anxious and more outgoing, though clearly intoxicated. Ron turned his gaze away from me, while nodding in agreement. I asked, "What are the main reasons for taking your un-prescribed medication?" Ron insisted, "I take my meds to calm my nerves." I reflected back, "It sounds like you are using alcohol and possibly other drugs in an effort to reduce stress?" Ron once again nodded. I shared, "The difficulty with that strategy is that it's only a temporary fix. Not only does your anxiety come back, but also you're on a roller coaster of coming down and needing to take more to get back up." I then asked, "Does that sound accurate?" Ron replied, "It's a dilemma, but there are no easy answers when I feel this way." I said, "Maybe down the road we could figure out some other options." I then suggested that if Ron could get out of the chaotic environment of the shelter he may feel safer and more secure. Ron immediately agreed with this evident point, so I went on to discuss some local transitional settings that would be far quieter than the shelter. Ron did not respond immediately, so I added that if he wanted more information we could arrange a tour or that I would be happy to share more of the details. Ron politely reminded me that he preferred to focus on getting housed as soon as possible and didn't want to get sidetracked, so we completed two more housing applications. During this time, Ron shared that he was a non-combat veteran. This was important information because it entitled him to priority status for at least one or two project-based subsidies. Before departing, Ron and I agreed to meet again in an effort to fill out at least one more application, as well as to consider future income options so he could eventually pay rent. Our discussion of income in relation to housing search seemed like a natural progression, and much less forced than my initial attempts of bringing up social security and welfare in a vacuum. We appeared to be on the right road now that housing was our main focus. At the same time, there was some initial success in framing a dilemma around Ron's anxiety level and his inclination to use alcohol and drugs. Similarly, this particular health issue will have more power and resonance if it can be framed in regard to future housing and income considerations.

The following day I saw Ron sitting and rocking in the waiting area of my office. He appeared oblivious to his surroundings as he laughed and muttered to himself. We immediately started on another housing form, despite my initial inclination to focus on his mental status and asking clinically relevant questions. This was a judgment call, but I thought that it was important to deal with the housing issue first, before bringing up other issues. Once the application was filled out, I asked if he had any thoughts on how to establish an income, so he could afford to pay rent. Ron shrugged his shoulders, looked down, and quietly said, "I've bothered you enough. There is no use continuing with this." I quickly replied, "Ron, through my work I've met many people who have felt like giving up, yet we've been able to secure income and housing. It may take a little time, but I know that we can do this!" Ron did not immediately respond. Instead he remained silent, while averting his eyes toward the floor. What Ron didn't know was that I was a bit taken aback by both his statement and his prolonged silence. I realized that this was part of Ron's pattern of withdrawing from things. Most likely it was his way to avoid uncomfortable topics, which often resulted in him feeling stuck and helpless. My next response was an artful and supportive confrontation to his avoidance. I said, "We can definitely resolve the income issue. I just need your help in figuring out whether it makes sense to find a job or to apply for benefits... Can we figure that out together?" Ron looked up and nodded.

Contract Implementation — Preparation and Action Phases

Ron and I had now successfully contracted to work toward attaining an income and affordable housing. At our next meeting I highlighted that we already had five housing applications pending with priority status due to his history of military service. If we could establish an income, we would be well on our way. With that in mind, Ron agreed to partake in an assessment of his job history and his current ability to gain meaningful employment. It was clear to me that his mental status was greatly compromised and very likely to interfere with his ability to work. Yet, I really didn't know Ron's perspective. This was my opportunity to gauge Ron's level of insight. More importantly, our joint assessment would give me a window into Ron's world, as well as help us to develop a mutual understanding on how to best proceed.

We met for almost an hour. As I like to say, we finally had our session! Ron told his story. He shared that he came from a large family and grew up in Mattapan, MA. He had three brothers and two sisters and they were no longer in communication. He felt very close to his mother, but now that he was older he didn't want to be a bother to her. He did not want her to worry about his troubles. He'd never been close with his father. His mom and dad had separated when he was very young. His most salient childhood memories were of him being constantly teased by others and often beaten by his brothers or other neighborhood kids. He constantly lived in fear and was very anxious about what would happen to him. He graduated high school and attended a year of community college, before feeling overwhelmed, falling behind and dropping out. His work history consisted of approximately two years in the army, before he achieved an honorable discharge due to issues with stress. Afterward, he worked in various manual labor jobs such as factory work, with his longest job lasting 10 months. He rented a room from time to time and lived with a girlfriend for almost a year before they broke up. This led to his current episode of homelessness. He'd been homeless for at least 5 years and had occasionally done some day labor, but it had been at least 6 years since he'd held a steady job. He reported being a loner, because he felt safer that way.

I thanked Ron for being so forthright and reflected that it sounded like he'd been on a difficult road. Sensing a strong connection, I took a chance and said, "You have had to deal with a great deal of fear and anxiety with no easy answers. Perhaps we could talk a little more about what type of stress and anxiety you've experienced and how your habit of taking un-prescribed medications began?" This led to an extended discussion that took place over our next two meetings. Ron shared his difficulties with addiction. He specifically talked about having drunk too much since his early teen years, as well as smoking crack. He reported that his crack use had been particularly frequent about six months ago, but he had since slowed down. Ron also expressed his deep-seated anxiety and fear of others, his inability to deal with social situations, and his need to be alone. He described full blown symptoms of panic that he had experienced since high school and prior to his drug and alcohol use. By the end of our session, we were in agreement to consider other ways of managing stress apart from alcohol and drug use. We also agreed that he would apply for Social Security benefits (SSI/SSDI), as well as Emergency Assistance funds from the Welfare Department. Fortunately, Ron already had a primary physician who could assist by signing off on the disability verification(s) needed to attain benefits. We made plans for a follow up meeting to finish filling out forms, as well as to consider other approaches for managing stress and anxiety. This was done, while highlighting that once Ron established an income, we'd begin a round of phone calls to check on the status of his recently submitted housing applications.

I now understood that Ron valued his safety and was very conscious of his isolation from others. He presented with significant anxiety, as well as avoidant personality characteristics. This is consistent with a history of trauma. His mental status also showed evidence of a thought disorder, though he had never directly confirmed having any delusions or auditory hallucinations. Things were further complicated by his evident addiction to crack and alcohol. While I wanted to get him housed as soon as possible, I was concerned that his level of drug use and psychiatric symptoms would compromise his ability to stay housed and to feel safe with neighbors. The dilemma was that we were considering independent housing options, yet we lacked access to support services and Ron had not yet begun treatment. However, I was aware of a transitional housing program with supports that specialized with homelessness and co-occurring disorders of addiction and mental illness. Figuring that Ron was a good match for this program, I planned to bring this up at our next meeting. We had now developed a playground of common language. Ron was initially comfortable with the word "un-prescribed medication" and was now directly discussing drug and alcohol use inclusive of crack. He also expressed a solid vocabulary of mental health terminology such as "anxiety," "stress" and "fear." Finally, I knew that he valued safety, so I planned to frame my offer as a way of feeling more secure and less fearful, while waiting for subsidized housing.

As the leaves turned from red and yellow to a uniform brown, we met again at my office and completed applications for income benefits. Upon completion, I asked Ron to consider meeting with folks at a local mental health clinic so he could get some relief from anxiety and stress. I highlighted that this would also help him to secure Social Security Income as quickly as possible. My offer resonated well in Ron's world, so he quickly agreed to the plan. Feeling a bit exuberant by my initial success, I explained to Ron that attaining a subsidized housing placement was most likely a few months away, and so he might feel safer waiting for housing in a more supportive and quieter environment such as a transitional housing program. Ron intuitively picked up on the word "program" and adamantly refused. He began pulling away before I could even begin to divulge that it consisted of specialized programming for dually diagnosed individuals. At that moment I realized, if we were going to get anywhere, we needed to try independent housing first.

Over the next two weeks Ron began receiving welfare money and completed an intake at a local mental health clinic that specialized in trauma and anxiety disorders. We began some initial work around strengthening his coping skills, as well as more freely discussing his addiction issues and its impact on his mental and physical health. Within this context, I once again brought up transitional housing with support services as an interim option. I carefully avoided the word "program," while explaining the different mental health and substance abuse services offered. Ronald listened intently before indicating that he appreciated the offer, but was not comfortable attending groups. He re-affirmed his need for help, but clearly stated that he was not ready to do more. Although I still wondered if he had a thought disorder and felt concerned about his addiction, I was happy to see him begin outpatient treatment. It took about three months, but we were now off and running with housing applications pending, a source of income established, and pertinent treatment.

Housing First

On a frigid late November morning, Ron received a letter from the local housing authority requesting an interview and instructing him to bring ID and proof of income. Ron had been offered subsidized housing! Ron appeared teary eyed and said that he was extremely grateful for all my help. He then looked down and said, "There is something that I should tell you. I am not sure if you will believe me, but I don't feel right keeping it a secret any longer." He then looked up and said, "There's a reason why I've been homeless for so long!" I replied, "You mean something different from what we've already discussed?" Nodding, Ronald continued, "Think of it this way, if you had valuable information... I mean something really valuable like the cure to a deadly disease. What would others do to bring you down?" Bewildered, yet calm, I replied, "What do you mean?" Ron went on to explain, "About five years ago I stumbled upon the cure for AIDS. I can't share too much, but believe me… it's a miraculous cure that is derived from pure sunlight. Now, certain individuals who have some sway with the churches and the police are not happy about this. They've dedicated multiple resources in an effort to silence me. They are involved in nefarious activities meant to bring me down and take away the cure!" I made eye contact and responded, "Ron… I really appreciate how hard it must have been to share such personal details. I am truly taken aback by what you've been going through. My role is to help you to feel safe and to deal with the stress in your life, as well as support your transition to housing. What you shared is really helpful because it gives me a better understanding of your world and the day to day challenges that you face." Ron appreciated my response and the session ended with a much greater sense of connection than we'd had through our previous meetings. The progress we made toward housing played a pivotal role. It opened the door to a greater level of trust and sharing, while also alerting me to what appeared to be a fixed delusional system. Understanding Ron's world, I was able to express, in a sensitive manner, the importance of us sharing at least some of this information with his therapist, so she could help him to manage his stress and anxiety in regard to these issues. I also added that this information may help him to qualify for social security benefits, so we might want to revise his application. In the meantime, he could continue to collect Emergency Assistance money from the department of welfare.

With the New Year rapidly approaching, it had finally happened. Ron not only moved into his own apartment, but he also qualified for social security benefits (SSI/SSDI)! While I was extremely excited to hear the news, this was not the end of our work but a new beginning. Some questions remained:

- Would Ron consistently pay his rent or would his money get spent on drugs or alcohol?
- Would he feel safe and secure in his new apartment or would he end up leaving the apartment due to paranoid delusions?
- Is it safe to move someone with severe mental illness and untreated substance abuse issues into an independent apartment?

Fortunately, Ron remained dedicated to our weekly office visits. Now that he had a safe place to sleep, shower, and shave, Ron looked like he had done a makeover, appearing well groomed and neatly dressed. Further, his recent sharing of his medical research and the plots to bring him down seemed therapeutic. Ron no longer felt alone in his fight for safety and freedom. This level of engagement and trust was critical because Ron could end our relationship and thereby cut himself off from needed support at any time. All he had to do was not answer the door and stop attending appointments. This was independent housing and not part of a program that required ongoing apartment visits or participation treatment. This was the original *housing first*! During our first meeting at his new residence, we discussed some of the challenges inherent to achieving a stable place to live. Ron clearly understood his responsibilities of paying rent and taking care of his apartment. We also discussed his level of comfort with neighbors and developed a safety or crisis plan in case he ran into any difficulties. Predictably, major difficulties ensued.

The following day, Ron showed up at my office and appeared distraught. He handed me a letter he had just received from Social Security. It stated that he needed a payee and was not allowed to directly receive his funds. I had originally recommended this because establishing a payee guaranteed rent payment, while limiting the amount of money that could be spent on drugs and alcohol. Ron did not agree with this recommendation, but we were still able to make a plan on how to institute a payee and I promised to help him devise a budget that would include a weekly spending allotment. I also highlighted that we could get a doctor to sign off on his ability to manage his own funds, but that was not apt to succeed unless we addressed the level of his drug and alcohol intake. Ron left our meeting with a sense of ambivalence. Even though he was able to see the advantages of having a virtually guaranteed rent payment, he felt disrespected and infantilized. I doubt he left with any increased motivation to address substance abuse issues, but perhaps important seeds were planted for future conversations in regard to his addiction and how it limited his options. Thankfully, we agreed to meet again in order to devise a budget plan and to further support the transition to his new apartment. However, Ron soon became less receptive to home visits and much more protective of his privacy.

Over the next two months, Ron reported major problems with unwelcomed houseguests and his mental status had significantly deteriorated. He still showed up regularly for our appointments, but he was often inebriated, as well as more withdrawn and depressed. Further, he was now willing to discuss his alcohol and drug intake in more detail, but unwilling to consider going to a detoxification facility, which he desperately needed. Ron stated that he could not imagine dealing with groups and being confined to a unit. His treatment team via the local mental health clinic had recently begun Ron on a trial of psychotropic medications. These meds were prescribed to help level out Ron's mood and to alleviate psychotic symptoms, but did little to reduce his social anxiety. Ron experienced these medications as a major step toward reducing stress and helping him to sleep through the night. The treatment team understood the importance of addressing Ron's anxiety symptoms without prescribing addictive medications such as benzodiazepines (e.g., Valium). Therefore, an anti-depressant that had shown some effectiveness at reducing anxiety symptoms was under consideration. Ron also agreed to continue counseling sessions that focused on enhancing his coping skills, as well as developing cognitive-behavioral techniques for reducing stress. However well intended, the effectiveness of this treatment approach was severely hampered by Ron's continued dependence on crack and alcohol. Similarly, our efforts of transitioning him from homelessness to housing were about to hit a serious roadblock.

Almost three months had passed since Ron had moved into his apartment and our meetings had become much less frequent. Early one morning Ron arrived at my office, and asked to meet with a sense of urgency. He appeared a bit gaunt and was grasping a letter in his trembling hands. It was a letter of eviction for disturbing his neighbors and for illegal drug use. Ron then went on to express, with considerable shame and frustration, how out of control things had gotten. Over the past month his drug use had dramatically increased, and the people distributing the drugs began staying at his apartment throughout the day and sometimes overnight. When they were in his apartment, they would play loud music, get high, and eat his food. He was afraid to share this with anyone due to the continued threats of retribution. If he kept the door locked and refused to let people in, they just kept on knocking throughout the night. Due to the continuous loud knocking and music, his neighbors called the police. When the police arrived they cleared the apartment of unwelcomed guests, but also gave Ron a notice to appear in court for drug possession, which was not on his person, but nevertheless in his apartment. Fortunately, he was not immediately put in jail, but now had to respond to a court summons. Ron, who had successfully avoided the police and others for so long, was now in a real fix. He could no longer "not be a bother" by simply avoiding others. He was now forced to confront things in court or lose his housing and go to jail.

Remarkably, in Ron's mind the unwelcomed houseguests and the police had conspired against him. He thought that they worked for a wider network of powerful people who were assigned to discredit him and his cure for AIDS, so pharmaceutical companies could continue to profit by selling drugs to chronically ill people. This resulted in Ron and I discussing ways to better assure his safety and how continued drug use left him confused, defenseless and an easy mark for others to take advantage of. The present context of a pending eviction interpreted through the lens of a paranoid delusion jibed well with his need to think clearly so he could better defend himself. In that moment Ron had connected to the discrepancy between his overindulgence on drugs and his ability to remain safe. Hoping to build some motivation and gumption I stated, "Ron, if you want to keep your apartment and stay out of jail, then you need to prove that you are actively addressing these issues noted in the letter." What I recommended was for Ron to enter a detoxification facility that specialized in dual diagnosis issues followed by a step down or transitional program. I mentioned that I knew the staff at the detox and they would be sensitive to his level of anxiety. Ron was now contemplative, but wanted time to think things over. We planned to meet the next day.

The following morning, Ron showed up at my office uncharacteristically early and was carrying a small black backpack full of clothes. Before I could say a word, Ron said, "I am ready to go!" We then made arrangements to get him into a detoxification program for dually diagnosed individuals. Even though Ron struggled with his anxiety on a daily basis, he managed to stay 12 full days. He left the detoxification facility in time to attend his court hearing. Because this was Ron's first offense coupled with his recent completion of a detoxification program, the judge was convinced to continue the case for six months without a finding. The judge stated that Ron needed to report back to the court without any new charges, as well as clear evidence of sobriety. If Ron succeeded, then the charges would be dropped. Unfortunately the housing authority was not as sympathetic. They stated that Ron needed to leave the premises, or he would end up in housing court. Upon receiving this news Ron took off and began drinking heavily for several days. Approximately one week later I knocked on Ron's apartment door and he agreed to meet. He appeared depressed and close to tears. He was now at a crossroads where every decision carried the full weight of major life consequences. I said, "Ron, it's not too late to turn things around. We have the opportunity to get your court case dismissed!" Ron sadly replied, "What's the difference, if I am going to lose my housing." In an attempt to revive hope, I said, "If you were to voluntarily leave this apartment, we can get a future housing subsidy. I know of transitional housing options that will help you gain sobriety, while addressing issues of stress and anxiety. Not only would you get away from people who have tormented you, but you could graduate from a transitional residential setting to independent housing placement." Ron appeared to be listening as evidenced by his biting his lip and renewing eye contact. He then weakly said, "I guess we can give it a try." Reassuringly, I responded, "This will look great in the eyes of the court and will qualify you for a new housing subsidy."

After our careful deliberation, Ron was willing to enter a transitional residence for people with co-occurring disorders. This meant that he needed to once again enter a detoxification facility, because the transitional residence, which was relapse tolerant, required initial sobriety upon entrance. Ron now knew that he was capable of completing the detox and understood that his future housing and freedom were at stake. He therefore entered the detox program without major objection. Interestingly enough, this was the same detox facility and transitional residence that I had suggested many months prior. Back then, Ron did not have the motivation and I did not have the leverage to convince him otherwise. Over time, our relationship grew and the words, ideas, and values associated with treatment were no longer foreign or threatening. Undoubtedly my willingness to house him first, rather than insist on residential treatment programs, played a central role in establishing a trusting relationship, as well as helping Ron to understand that I respected his autonomy. This provided a positive and safe relationship for jointly considering restricted options set forth by the courts and housing authority. A housing first approach provided Ron with the opportunity to learn by doing and sometimes failing, as opposed to being indefinitely stuck or stymied. Only, this time he wasn't alone and homeless. Together, we could face these difficulties with the hope of a better future. It was during these moments of crisis that important insights were reached and life-changing decisions were made within the confines of a trusting and safe relationship. After approximately ten months of working together, Ron entered a residential program with a new-found understanding of the importance of achieving sobriety, even if a true sense of recovery still eluded him.

Ron spent six challenging months at the transitional residence. We continued to meet weekly at my office with the goal of helping him to adjust, as well as to consider future housing options. For the most part, Ron maintained his sobriety, though he contemplated leaving the residence on several occasions due to his perceived mistreatment by staff. Upon Ron's request, I stepped in on more than one occasion to serve as a mediator. In the end, Ron not only completed the transitional residential program, but his court case was also dismissed. In addition he found a self-help group that he really liked at the local *Social Club* program that served adults with major mental illnesses. Finally, Ron accepted a referral to the Department of Mental Health for case management services and was placed in permanent subsidized housing with ongoing support services. The support service consisted of monthly case coordination and a weekly home visit. Once community based supports were fully in place, Ron and I agreed to formally end our working relationship. Several months later, Ronald dropped by to say hello and thanked me for our successful journey. He then proudly showed me his first paycheck in almost five years. The *Social Club* had provided Ron with a job counselor who had helped him to find part-time employment that was allowable via social security (SSDI) regulations. Ron was now working as a messenger in downtown Boston, and resided in a subsidized apartment with support services. He also felt a real sense of belonging at the local *Social Club*. Truly amazed at all he had accomplished, I wished him well and grinned, knowing that there were valuable lessons learned by both of us.

Lessons Learned

This is one of many original housing first narratives. During the 1980s I remember advocates chanting, "Housing is Treatment!" Prior to the current *housing first* movement, outreach workers across the country undoubtedly tried its many variants. The following are the lessons learned as reflected in *Ronald's Narrative*, as well as from our multiple experiences with implementing a housing first philosophy.

- The same principles of outreach counseling (pretreatment perspective) apply whether we are working with someone who is homeless or living in a housing first apartment.
- Offering *housing first* is consistent with the overarching and guiding tenet of outreach, which is to "meet the clients where they are at."

- Attach affordable housing resources directly to outreach teams in order to provide better and quicker access for homeless individuals.
- It is critical for outreach workers and/or case managers, who know the client best, to support transition into housing.
- On call and rapid response teams are needed for addressing client crisis issues (psychiatric, addiction, and medical) and housing crisis issues such as resolving major conflicts with neighbors, property destruction, and non-payment of rent.
- Establishing a good and effective communication with landlords is essential toward addressing housing issues and conflicts prior and/or during a housing crisis.
- Rapid re-housing is important toward ultimate success, but the new housing is not necessarily independent housing.
- Both affordable housing resources and support services are essential elements for promoting housing stabilization.

Pioneers, such as Dr. Sam Tsemberis, Ph.D. (Executive Director of Pathways to Housing), have done much to research, formalized and popularized *housing first* as an effective strategy toward ending homelessness among certain homeless subgroups. *Housing first* is not a panacea for homelessness and poverty. This is a complex issue that encompasses economic and social concerns such as high unemployment, low wages, and the availability of affordable housing stock. However, we do know that it is an effective way for serving the most vulnerable of homeless individuals. People who are among the long term and episodically homeless, while suffering from major mental illnesses and other disabling conditions, are in dire need of quick access to housing with support services that are guided by pretreatment principles of care. I believe that most people understand or can be persuaded that *housing first* is the right strategy to help this extremely vulnerable homeless subgroup.

If we are to be successful in either ending or significantly reducing chronic homelessness, than we must not only have access to a wide range of affordable housing options, but also quality outreach and housing stabilization services that effectively apply pretreatment principles of care. Ultimately, the formation of a trusting relationship that promotes safety and supports critical transitions to affordable housing, while developing goals and motivation to create positive change is central to our mission. Our hope is to restore health and housing for those who are most in need.

Stages of Engagement

Ecological Phase	Developmental Stage	Intervention
Pre-Engagement	Trust vs. Mistrust Issues of Safety	Observe, Identify Potential Client, Respect Personal Space, Assess Safety, Attempt Verbal & Non-Verbal Communication, Offer Essential Need Item, Listen for Client Language, Establish Initial Communication, etc.
Engagement	Trust vs. Mistrust Issues of Dependency Boundary Issues	Communicate with Empathy & Authenticity, Learn Client Language, Identify & Reinforce Client Strengths, Provide Unconditional Regard, Avoid Power Struggles, Emphasis on Joining the resistance, Introduction of Roles, Begin & Continue development of Healthy Boundaries, Establish On-going Communication, etc.
Contracting	Autonomy vs. Shame Issues of Control Initiative vs. Guilt	Further Define Roles & Boundaries, Universalize Human Frailty, Negotiate Reachable Goals, Explore Client History in relation to stated goals, Determine Eligibility for Potential Resources & Services that interests the client, Further Define Shared Objectives by Utilizing Client Language, Education re: Symptom Management, Review & Reinforce Current Coping Strategies, Jointly Consider Housing Options, etc.

* Many of the interventions listed are applicable to various phases (stages) of the outreach process, yet have particular relevance to the indicated phase.

Concepts from Germain and Gitterman's (1980) Life Model and Eric Erickson's (1968) Psychosocial Developmental Model influenced the formation of the above table.

Helping the Homeless

[Ernest Dempsey is the Editor of *Recovering The Self: The Journal of Hope and Healing.* The following interview is excerpted from RTS Vol. III, No. 2]

Jay S. Levy's recently published book *Homeless Narratives & Pretreatment Pathways: From Words to Housing* (Loving Healing Press, 2010) is about homelessness and the issues related to outreach counseling, case management, and advocacy for long-term and episodically homeless individuals. Jay's book presents real-life narratives of homeless people with whom the author worked to help with housing, care, and treatment. The book discusses several key points involved in successful transition of people from homelessness to housing, and afterward.

Ernest: Hello Jay! It's the first time for me to talk to an expert about homelessness. Now, the general view of a homeless person is one who lives in the open and can't financially afford living in a house. Is that correct?

Jay: Firstly, thanks for the opportunity to discuss the important issue of homelessness. This is a very broad issue and the word "homeless" can encompass many things. It refers to individuals as well as to families. People are considered homeless if they are residing at a shelter, or outside, or in a vehicle, or any place that is normally not meant for human habitation. Some definitions of homelessness include the large numbers of people doubled up or couch surfing... adults or families who have no home of their own, but are dependent upon others for shelter. The HUD definition of homelessness does not include this large number of doubled up persons and is more restricted to counting people who are living outside or residing in homeless shelters. As you've mentioned, there is almost always a financial issue that intersects with any homeless situation, but the reasons and causes of homelessness are numerous.

Ernest: So, as we speak here, how many people are homeless in America?

Jay: There are various estimates and counts that are different due to either the definition of homelessness or the methodology used. Every year, HUD authorizes a point in time count that is done by the various continuums of care (regional networks) across the nation. The 2009 count reports over 643,000 persons, which is composed of approximately 63% individuals and 37% families and children. It is a one-night snapshot of homelessness, so the number is far less than reflected in the yearly count (HUD AHAR, 2010) that estimates over 1.5 million people seeking shelter. This includes the vast majority of short-term homeless folks who use the shelter on a temporary basis, while in between jobs and relationships, or for some other reason lack access to income or affordable housing. Also, it should be noted that the vast majority of adults that comprise homeless families are women, while homeless single adults are predominantly men. When you factor in the unsheltered population throughout an entire year or other definitions of homelessness, the estimates range from 2.3 to 3.5 million people who are homeless annually (Burt and Aron).

A researcher by the name of Dennis Culhane has shared some important data that indicates that over a one year period; approximately 80% of individuals experiencing homelessness are in shelters on a short-term basis due to temporary setbacks often resulting from job loss, disruption of critical supports, and lack of access to housing. In fact, our observations (among outreach workers) have confirmed that the vast majority of homeless persons very quickly cycle in and out of homelessness. That being said, jobs have really dried up and the economic tailspin has led to greater than nine percent unemployment. This has already negatively impacted family homelessness, where the numbers have steadily risen over the past couple of years and there is concern that a similar trend may be now occurring with individuals.

Ernest: What are some other reasons besides financial fragility that render people homeless in America?

Jay: Many contributing factors go beyond income and affordable housing issues. What we find among homeless individuals is a range of functioning levels, as well as chronic medical, substance abuse, and mental health issues, all part of the picture in conjunction with poverty and lack of affordable housing. Trauma and homelessness are clearly interlocked. What one experiences in order to become homeless can be emotionally devastating. The lasting effects may or may not warrant the DSM diagnosis of Post Traumatic Stress Disorder, but their impacts remain profound and enduring. Sub-groups among the long-term homeless have experienced trauma at different levels. In fact, it is not unusual to meet homeless persons who have experienced layered trauma from an array of traumatic events. Veterans account for at least 13% of homeless individuals in America (HUD AHAR, 2010, p. 16), and many have experienced combat trauma. While less frequent, it is not unusual to meet homeless men and women, with foster care histories, who report profound physical and/or sexual trauma during their childhoods. Further, others have sustained traumatic brain injury (TBI). An impact brain injury can cause major functional impairment, as well as significant psychological difficulty from the traumatic event that caused it. In addition, the high occurrence of substance abuse among homeless individuals (HUD AHAR, 2010, p. 22) and the associated lack of judgment and unstable relationships can result in the increased likelihood of witnessing or directly experiencing personal violence. This is especially true when you consider the unsafe living conditions that homeless persons often endure. The numbers of people who are homeless and have experienced trauma are significant, and so it is vital that a trauma-informed approach is adopted and consistently utilized. Finally, it should be noted that one of the main causes of homelessness is institutional discharges. Whether it be from foster care, the hospitals (mental health & medical), or the jails, people are discharged on a daily basis into homelessness without access to affordable housing and without adequate follow up plans.

The long-term homeless are comprised of unaccompanied adults and couples who have been homeless for a year or more, as well as folks who have experienced multiple episodes of homelessness. Many of these people suffer from chronic medical issues, mental illness and addictions, as well as from not having a home. We call this group the chronically homeless, and this is where my expertise and interest converge. A significant percentage of this group consists of highly vulnerable people and unfortunately, every year many of them die from untreated illness and/or exposure to the elements. Our mission is to reach out to long-term homeless individuals and to build pathways to housing and needed treatment. My book tells the stories of different people experiencing long-term homelessness and gives an intricate view of the challenges inherent in building these pathways. In many instances, the outreach worker and client go on a figurative and literal journey in pursuit of housing, stability, and a better quality of life. That's why my book is entitled *Homeless Narratives & Pretreatment Pathways: From Words to Housing*. I want to get beyond the numbers and tell people's stories in an effort to provide a better connection between policy, programs, clinical approaches, and what people are really experiencing on the ground.

Ernest: I assume the homeless are more vulnerable to accidents and diseases. What kinds of threats/misfortunes are these homeless people generally prone to, from your experience?

Jay: The world of a person experiencing homelessness is fraught with challenges to their safety and it is not unusual to witness or experience violence. Many homeless individuals avoid the shelters due to fear for their own safety or concerns about their belongings being stolen. However, there is a catch 22 because if you stay outside in areas that either get exceedingly cold or hot, you are at risk of issues ranging from dehydration and heat stroke to frostbite and hypothermia. Many of the homeless we meet suffer from chronic untreated medical conditions. A national survey of homeless providers and their clients (Burt, et al. 1999, p. xix) found that 46% of these clients report chronic health conditions such as arthritis, cancer, diabetes, liver disease, HIV/AIDS, etc. These health issues, as well as chronic mental illness and addiction, are only exacerbated by unsafe, substandard living conditions that lack basic access to food, clean clothes, sanitary bathroom facilities, and a secure place to sleep. Additional research (Hwang et al., 1998; Hwang, 2000) shows that adults who are homeless and unsheltered for at least 6 months are at high risk of death if they fit one or more of the following criteria: age above 60, three or more visits to the emergency room during the prior 3 months, triple diagnosed (major mental illness, substance abuse, medical illness), history of frostbite and/or hypothermia or immersion foot, other medical conditions — cirrhosis, heart failure, renal failure. When one considers the impact of unstable and chaotic environments on health issues, it's hard to fathom why healthcare professionals and residential programs serving at-risk homeless individuals have often prioritized compliance with treatment above housing placement. It is clear that successful treatment is often dependent upon living conditions that promote, rather than diminish, health and safety. This is one of the main reasons why housing first initiatives and harm reduction approaches are vital to successfully addressing long term homelessness.

Ernest: Okay Jay, tell us a little about the resources and services available to a person experiencing homelessness.

Jay: I have found that many people in the homeless community are very savvy as to where to find needed resources and services. The outreach worker is well served to use this naturally evolving community resource base, in addition to surfing the Internet or abiding by local service directories. That being said, one of the more important tasks of outreach work is to help people to become acquainted and eligible for the array of basic services and resources that are available, as well as serve as a guide through the bureaucratic maze that one inevitably encounters. It is critical that homeless persons are able to access what they need in order to survive and move beyond homelessness. Most major urban centers such as Washington DC, New York City, and Boston provide access to meal programs, shelters, Department of Transitional Assistance (DTA), Social Security offices, and housing authorities, as well as other homeless providers. However, smaller urban centers and rural areas often lack needed resources, making it difficult to find basic things like food and shelter. In addition, public transportation is often not available to help people reach more resource and service rich areas.

At the other end of the spectrum, one of the more exciting developments has been the promulgation of *housing first* alternatives. A housing first approach recognizes that the critical intervention is to house people as rapidly as possible, while simultaneously offering support services, but not require treatment as a *prerequisite* to getting housed. This approach has shown some initial success by demonstrating housing retention and reducing the financial costs associated with homelessness (Stefancic and Tsemberis, 2007). Out in Western MA, where I work, and many other places, such as Denver, NYC, and Boston, we have begun providing affordable housing alternatives with support services that long-term homeless persons can easily access as long as they're agreeable to taking on the challenges of paying rent, getting along with neighbors, and taking care of their apartment. There is some compelling evidence that housing First Programs have not only reduced financial costs and the numbers of unsheltered long-term homeless individuals, but have also saved people's lives. Many of the long-term homeless are untreated while suffering from major mental illnesses, addictions, and chronic medical issues. They often lack the necessary insight and judgment to accept needed treatment services unless they are first housed and then provided with the opportunity to gradually build trusting relationships with service providers. *Housing first* can and does eventually lead to treatment, while keeping people safe from the elements. It is the ultimate harm reduction program.

Ernest: *Homeless Narratives & Pretreatment Pathways* is mainly about how to approach and work with individuals who are either difficult to engage or are experiencing long-term homelessness. So what is meant by "Pretreatment" and what is its significance?

Jay: I have found that a treatment bias tends to permeate throughout the network of homeless services and resources that many folks need. This basic sensibility is around the concept of "readiness." This could be in conjunction to receiving appropriate clinical care such as counseling services or in relation to being accepted to various housing programs that also provide support services. Many people are deemed "not yet ready" and therefore not provided access to services and resources that they so desperately need. Further, I've found that even well-schooled clinicians seem to have difficulty with the idea of being present with a client and solidifying the relationship, as opposed to moving directly into treatment issues. Similarly, my experience with paraprofessional staff working in the shelters is that they very quickly move to referring clients to resources and services without really understanding a person's story and what could really help. In contrast, a pretreatment approach follows the social work edict of starting "where clients are at." The client is always ready, but we may have to adjust our approach to do productive work with the client. In order to inform the worker or clinician, the book presents five guiding principles of clinical care for doing pretreatment. This includes understanding the phases of engagement, stages of Common Language Development, Ecological Considerations (transition and adaptation issues), addressing issues of Safety via crisis intervention and harm reduction approaches, as well as facilitating the Change Process. This approach is particularly useful when working with long-term or episodic homeless persons or other hard-to-reach populations who are not initially interested in treatment and are reticent to request help of any kind. When you view this approach in conjunction with homeless narratives, it also informs program design and homeless policy. In fact, the REACH Housing First Model that we developed in Western MA was based on this pretreatment model.

Ernest: By the real-life narratives included in your book, we see that some people are recalcitrant to being housed and are at risk of returning to their homeless lifestyle after they are provided with sheltered accommodation. Why does this happen?

Jay: Yes... the stories of Old Man Ray, Butch, Lacey, and others speak to this important issue. There is more than one reason for this, but it basically falls into the following three major categories.

First, when working with a chronic homeless population or with people whose day-to-day functioning is significantly compromised by mental health, substance abuse, and/or medical issues, support services are instrumental toward promoting housing stabilization. Some people just don't have the level of skills and supports needed to maintain their housing. Sadly, support services are often underfunded and not available.

Second, issues with transition and adaptation play a major role. When people are homeless over a long period of time, they eventually adapt to their homeless situation. This may include giving up hope of ever being housed, specific behaviors and perceptions to meet immediacy needs (i.e. finding shelter, food or alcohol), and to derive meaning from their unsheltered existence such as valuing their freedom. Housing a person comes with new demands, expectations, and often lacks meaning. Once a certain amount of difficulty occurs due to interpersonal conflict (often issues of control), lack of rent payment, or with certain behavioral issues, it is often easier for the formerly homeless person to return to the streets; in other words, go back to familiar circumstances that are in better synch with their current thoughts and behaviors.

Third, acute issues and the lack of timely crisis intervention play a significant role. Many of the folks we house have untreated issues and lack the insight required to access treatment. We should expect that along with being housed, which is a significant change in environment, there will be an imminent need for crisis intervention. The more that we can take on this challenge and see it as an opportunity to promote awareness and access treatment, the more likely we will be successful in promoting housing stability and building an ongoing support network.

Ultimately, a pretreatment approach is critical because it guides outreach counselors, case managers and residential staff on the journey toward housing placement and stabilization with chronic homeless persons and other populations that are difficult to engage.

Ernest: What are the relative roles of psychologists and social workers in helping the homeless find a permanent place to live?

Jay: This is a great question! Generally speaking, Social Workers are trained from more of an Ecological Perspective where they take a "person in environment" approach, which is much broader than providing psychotherapy. However, many social workers provide outpatient counseling services in the same manner as many psychologists. One of the great frustrations is that both social workers and psychologists sometimes define their roles in a much too narrow fashion when working with the homeless or with those who are on the verge of losing their housing. Whether one is working with individuals or families, much depends on our clients having a stable place to live. This goes back to Maslow's Hierarchy of Needs. The main point is that once housing is lost, it is much more difficult to achieve and maintain stability, let alone work on some of the more profound issues via psychotherapy. Both psychologists and social workers need to fully appreciate this reality. This means that there are times when it is warranted to step back from the role of an outpatient therapist, and expand one's duties into advocacy and case management in an effort to help either find or maintain housing, or at very least, find a shelter and other essential resources.

Ernest: Developing a common language between the homeless and the helper has been underscored in your book. Are there any particular courses/trainings for developing such a language that helps in winning the subject's trust?

Jay: This is one of those basic yet overlooked areas. After all, developing a common language is our main tool for doing counseling, advocacy and case management. One of the things that make this book innovative is the case illustration and the intricate details that are provided around common language construction. I am drawing a great deal from Narrative Therapy, so I would think that any coursework or presentations on this subject would be helpful. There is a great book entitled *Narrative Therapy: The Social Construction of Preferred Realities* by Jill Freedman and Gene Combs. Also, there are some nice presentations on mediation and cultural diversity that should provide some focus on developing common language. Finally, there are some great online resources for research and information for working with the homeless through the National Healthcare for the Homeless Council's site http://www.nhchc.org/ and another fantastic Internet site is SAMHSA's Homeless Resource Center http://homeless.samhsa.gov/default.aspx.

Ernest: And what are some of the major roles that government and non-government entities can serve in helping the homeless in America?

Jay: Considering the reported difficulties of accessing resources, and services and the dizzying effects of needless bureaucracy, it is important to utilize what we have in the most efficient manner possible. Currently, Ten and Five Year Plans have been developed and implemented in an effort to end chronic homelessness, and thereby reduce social and financial costs (All Roads Lead Home, 2008; National Alliance to End Homelessness, 2000). Ultimately, these plans are based on collaborative efforts between concerned individuals, advocacy groups, local city and town employees, politicians, policy makers, non-profit service providers, charities, businesses, etc. These collaborative networks are being established to address fundamental issues such as developing affordable housing with support services, promoting better access to community-based resources and services, and implementing strategies of prevention in order to reduce future homelessness. Advocates and policy makers now understand that addressing access, resource and prevention issues are paramount, if we are to be successful in turning long-term homelessness into a rare or unusual phenomenon. This has culminated in the Obama Administration's recent unveiling of the first National Strategic Plan to Prevent and End Homelessness via the US Interagency Council on Homelessness during 2010. This plan declares support for *housing first* initiatives and continued interagency collaboration in an effort to make significant inroads with both families and individuals. While this is good news from the standpoint of new cooperative networks and more efficient use of resources, it does not directly address macroeconomic issues that impact unemployment, underemployment, and the lack of affordable housing.

Ernest: Tell me Jay, what can the layman do to help the homeless?

Jay: A number of things that can be done (See *7 Ways of Helping* list, p. 36). Many positive things can happen when there is a sense of caring and human contact. Get to know the names of some of the homeless persons you frequently meet in your daily travels or in your neighborhood. Don't be afraid to ask if they are getting any help or if there are any basic things they need. If you are wary of donating money directly to a person experiencing homelessness, consider giving them need items such as food, clothes, or even information regarding a nearby resource center. Many organizations accept financial donations. It's a pretty sure bet that organizations working for the homeless are financially strained. Consider donating, but doing so toward funding a specific cause such as providing rental assistance and supporting transitions to housing. Many other places like the Salvation Army or community resource centers accept donations of food, household items and clothes. Another nice way to contribute is by way of volunteer service. Currently, my daughter volunteers her time at a Survival Center that provides clothing, serves hot meals, and has a food pantry that serves our local community, which includes the homeless. Meal programs are often in need of volunteers to help prepare and serve meals to people who are struggling to make ends meet.

Ernest: For all interested readers, Jay, would you tell us who and/or where to reach for help in case some homeless person/family is noticed in search of help?

Jay: The key is to find out what are the homeless resources and services in your area. Every state has PATH programs that are funded by both state and federal dollars. PATH stands for Projects for Assistance in Transitions from Homelessness. The people in charge of these programs are very informed regarding homeless resources and services. Most states have funded various non-profits, so you want to locate the right service provider for your region. This can be done by going to the following website: http://pathprogram.samhsa.gov/Channel/Default.aspx.

Once you get to the PATH-SAMHSA website, just click on the "Grantees" tab and then you can do a search for the homeless service organization that serves your particular state and region. I work for Eliot CHS-Homeless Services and we are the sole PATH Provider serving Massachusetts. I am the regional manager for both Central and Western Massachusetts and have counterparts who manage the North East and South East regions of our state. Our program is listed on the PATH website and if someone were to call, we could direct them to critical resources and services.

Other places to look for help include the local Department of Transitional Assistance (DTA), where people can access Food Stamps, Emergency Assistance funds, and health insurance. Local DTA caseworkers normally have access to information on family and individual shelters and meal programs across the region that they cover. If that fails, an internet search under homeless shelters and/or meal programs for your particular area will most likely yield results. Finally, check your local phone directory under Social & Human Services, or inquire with your local church or synagogue. Places of faith are often quite involved with supporting community meal programs and other charitable efforts toward helping those who are most in need. Directing a homeless family or person to local resources and services can be the first critical step toward attaining critical assistance ranging from shelters and meals to healthcare and housing.

Ernest: Many thanks Jay for sharing your precious knowledge and taking time for this talk.

Jay: I appreciate you taking the time to interview me, and providing a forum for talking about these important issues. If anyone would like more information on my book including some recent reviews, please check out my website www.jayslevy.com. Thanks!

7 Ways of Helping

- Directly get to know people who are experiencing homelessness in your community and offer support by saying hello, introduce yourself and learn each others' names

- Offer a basic need item such as clothes (i.e. socks, hat, gloves, sweatshirt) directly to a person who lacks access to these items

- Identify helpful community resources such as food pantries, meal programs and shelters, and share this information with people without homes

- Volunteer your time at a community meal program, food pantry, or shelter, etc.

- Inquire with your local faith organizations and city/town officials as to what is currently being done to address homelessness and offer to assist by donating time, money, or helping to organize a fundraiser that is targeted toward a specific goal (e.g. Rental Assistance)

- Donate money or basic need items to non-profit or faith-based organizations whose mission is to help people without homes. Don't be afraid to try and target your donation toward a specific worthy goal such as providing rental assistance or supporting transitions to housing by paying for moving costs or needed household items, etc.

- Get politically involved, while educating yourself regarding current homeless policy on a local, state, and federal level

References

All Roads Lead Home, (2008). The Pioneer Valley's Plan to End Homelessness. Supported by the Cities of Holyoke, Northampton, Springfield, MA. Funded by One Family, Inc.

Burt, M.R.and Aron, L.Y. (2000). *America's homeless II: Populations and services.* Washington, DC: The Urban Institute.

Burt, M.R., Aron, L.Y., Douglas, T., Valente, J., Lee, E., Iwen, B. (1999, August). Homelessness: Programs and the people they serve. *Findings of a national survey of homeless assistance: 1996 summary report.* Washington, DC: The Urban Institute.

Culhane, D. P. and Metraux S. (2008, Winter). Rearranging the deck chairs or reallocating the life boats? *Journal of the American Planning Association,*Vol. 74, No. 1.

Dempsey, E. & Levy, J. S. (2010, October). Helping the homeless (interview). *Recovering The Self: A Journal of Hope and Healing,* II(4), pp. 74-81.

Epston, D., and White, M. (1992). *Experience, contradiction, narrative, and imagination: Selected papers of David Epston and Michael White, 1989-1991.* Adelaide, Australia: Dulwich Centre Publications.

Erikson, E.H. (1968). *Identity: youth and crisis.* New York: Norton.

Freedman, J., & Combs, G. (1996). *Narrative therapy: The social construction of preferred realities.* New York: W. W. Norton Company, Inc.

Germain, C.B., & Gitterman, A. (1980). *The life model of social work process.* New York: Columbia University Press.

Gladwell, M. (2006). Million Dollar Murray: Why problems like homelessness may be easier to solve than to manage. *The New Yorker,* February 13 & 20, 2006 edition.

Home and Healthy for Good Report (2010). Compiled by Massachusetts Housing & Shelter Alliance Staff. Retrieved from website: http://www.mhsa.net/matriarch/MultiPiecePageText.asp?PageID=60&PageName=HomeHealthyforGoodArchive

HUD Annual Homeless Report, (2010). 2009 Annual Homeless Assessment Report to Congress. Retrieved from website: http://www.hudhre.info/documents/5thHomelessAssessmentReport.pdf

Hwang, S.W., Lebow, J.J., Bierer, M.F., O'Connell, J., Orav, E.J., and Brennan, T.A.(1998). Risk factors for deaths in homeless adults in Boston. *Archives of Internal Medicine,* 158(13): 1454-1460.

Kuhn, R. and Culhane, D. P. (1998) Applying cluster analysis to test of a typology of homelessness: Results from the analysis of administrative data. *American Journal of Community Psychology* 17:1 , pp. 23-43.

Levy, J. S. (1998, Fall). Homeless outreach: A developmental model. *Psychiatric Rehabilitation Journal*, 22(2), pp. 123-131.

Levy, J. S. (2000, July-Aug.). Homeless outreach: On the road to pretreatment alternatives. *Families in Society: The Journal of Contemporary Human Services*, 81(4), pp. 360-368.

Levy, J. S. (2004). Pathway to a common language: A homeless outreach perspective. *Families in Society: The Journal of Contemporary Human Services*, 85(3), pp. 371-378.

Levy, J. S. (2010). Homeless narratives & pretreatment pathways: From words to housing. Ann Arbor, MI: Loving Healing Press.

Levy, J. S. (2011, July). The case for housing first: Moral, fiscal, and quality of life reasons for ending chronic homelessness. *Recovering The Self: A Journal of Hope and Healing*, III(3), pp. 45-51.

McKinney-Vento Program Eligibility Form (2002) HUD definition of Chronic Homelessness.

Miller, W.R. & Rollnick, S. (1991). *Motivational interviewing: Preparing people to change addictive behavior*. New York: Guilford.

National Alliance to End Homelessness (2000). *A plan not a dream: How to end homelessness in 10 years*. Retrieved from website:
www.endhomelessness.org/pub/tenyear/10yearplan.pdf.

O'Connell, J.J. *Premature Mortality in Homeless Populations: A Review of the Literature*, 19 pages. Nashville: National Health Care for the Homeless Council, Inc., 2005.

O'Connell, J.J, Swain S. Rough sleepers: A five year prospective study in Boston, 1999-2003. Presentation, Tenth Annual Ending Homelessness Conference, Massachusetts Housing and Shelter Alliance, Waltham, MA 2005.

Prochaska, J.O., & DiClemente, C.C. (1982). Trans theoretical therapy: Toward a more integrative model of change. *Psychotherapy: Theory, Research, and Practice*. 19, 276-288.

Stefancic, A., & Tsemberis, S. (2007, June). Housing first for long-term shelter dwellers with psychiatric disabilities in a suburban county: A four year study of housing access and retention. *The Journal of Primary Prevention*, 10.1007/s10935-007-0093-9, 15 pp.

Wasserman, J. A. and Clair, J. M. (2010). *At home on the street: People, poverty & a hidden culture of homelessness*. Boulder, Colorado: Lynne Rienner Publishers.

About the Author

Jay S. Levy has spent the last twenty-three years working with individuals who experience homelessness. He is the author of the highly acclaimed book *Homeless Narratives & Pretreatment Pathways: From Words to Housing* and has published several journal articles on the subject. He has helped to develop new *housing first* programs such as the Regional Engagement and Assessment for Chronically Homeless Housing First program (REACH). This was adopted by the Western Massachusetts Regional Network as an innovative approach toward reducing chronic homelessness and has also been integrated into the Pioneer Valley's 10-Year Plan to End Chronic Homelessness.

Jay received his MSW degree in clinical social work from Columbia University in 1988. He has achieved formal recognition from the Commonwealth of MA Department of Mental Health for his ongoing efforts to help under-served homeless individuals through his direct service, clinical supervision of staff, and program development. Jay is currently employed by Eliot CHS-Homeless Services as a Regional Manager for the statewide SAMHSA-PATH Homeless Outreach Program and Eliot's Western MA Housing First Program.

Jay lives in Western MA with his wife Louise and his two children, Talia and Sara. He is also an avid stargazer. Further information about homelessness, past and present publications, latest reviews, and interviews are available at his website: www.jayslevy.com

CPSIA information can be obtained at www.ICGtesting.com
Printed in the USA
BVOW07s1112190314

348112BV00004BA/103/P